Rockschool P0 8070 £10·67

Better Guitar With...
Rockschool

Welcome to Guitar Grade 4	2
Guitar Notation Explained	3
Pieces:	
Enough Said	4
Glide On Down	6
Hold On I'm Going	8
Rage Against Everything	10
Secret Place	12
There And Beck	14
Technical Exercises	16
Sight Reading	18
Improvisation & Interpretation	19
Ear Tests	20
General Musicianship Questions	21
The Guru's Guide	22
Entering Rockschool Exams	24

rockschool

www.rockschool.co.uk

Welcome To Guitar Grade 4

Welcome to the Rockschool Guitar Grade 4 pack. The book and CD contain everything needed to play guitar in this grade. In the book you will find the exam scores in both standard guitar notation and TAB. The accompanying CD has full stereo mixes of each tune, backing tracks to play along with for practice, tuning notes and spoken two bar count-ins to each piece. Handy tips on playing the pieces and the marking schemes can be found in the Guru's Guide on page 22. If you have any queries about this or any other Rockschool exam, please call us on **020 8332 6303**, email us at *info@rockschool.co.uk* or visit our website *www.rockschool.co.uk*. Good luck!

Level 2 Requirements for Grades 4 & 5

The nine Rockschool grades are divided into four levels. These levels correspond to the levels of the National Qualifications Framework (NQF). Further details about the NQF can be found at *www.qca.org.uk/NQF*. Details of all Rockschool's accredited qualifications can be found at *www.qca.org.uk/openquals*.

Guitar Grade 4 is part of Level 2. This Level is for those of you who are confident in all the key skills on guitar and who are stepping up to more advanced skills and stylistic expression.

Grade 4: in this grade you use a range of physical and expressive techniques with confidence, damping and the use of double stops and adjacent strings, legato and staccato, slides, fretting hand and whammy bar vibrato, hammer ons and pull offs, and accents, and you are experimenting with a range of dynamics from very quiet (pp) to very loud (ff). In this grade you are continuing to develop your ability to play with stylistic authority.

Grade 5: you will be confident in a range of physical and expressive techniques. You will be able to demonstrate your abilities across a number of styles and have control over tone and sound adjustments to suit the playing style of your choice.

Guitar Exams at Grade 4

There are **two** types of exam that can be taken using this pack: a Grade Exam and a Performance Certificate.

Guitar Grade 4 Exam: this is for players who want to develop performance and technical skills

Players wishing to enter for a Guitar Grade 4 exam need to prepare **three** pieces of which **one** may be a free choice piece chosen from outside the printed repertoire. In addition you must prepare the technical exercises in the book, undertake either a sight reading test or an improvisation & interpretation test, take an ear test and answer general musicianship questions. Samples of these tests are printed in the book along with audio examples on the CD.

Guitar Grade 4 Performance Certificate: this is for players who want to focus on performing in a range of styles

To enter for your Guitar Grade 4 Performance Certificate you play pieces only. You can choose any **five** of the six tunes printed in this book, or you can choose to bring in up to **two** free choice pieces as long as they meet the standards set out by Rockschool. Free choice piece checklists for all grades can be found on the Rockschool website: *www.rockschool.co.uk*.

Guitar Notation Explained

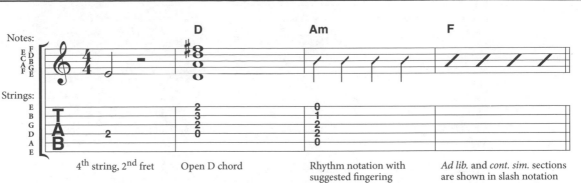

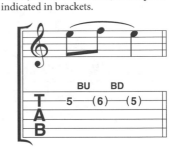
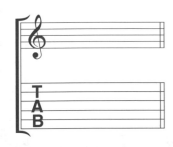
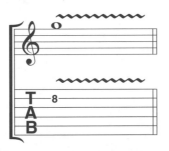

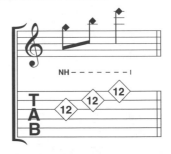
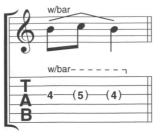
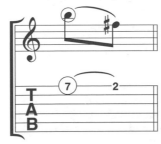
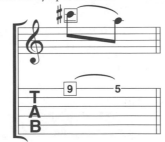
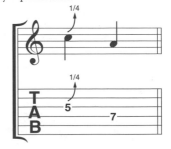
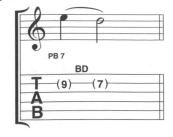
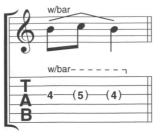

Enough Said

Hussein Boon

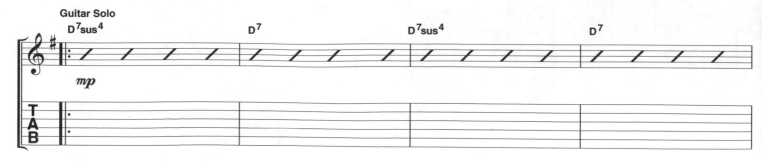

© 2006 Rock School Ltd.

Glide On Down

Joe Bennett

Hold On I'm Going

Steve Wrigley

Rage Against Everything

Deirdre Cartwright

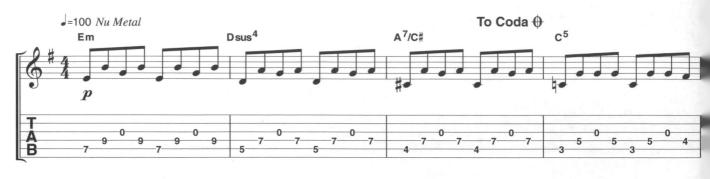

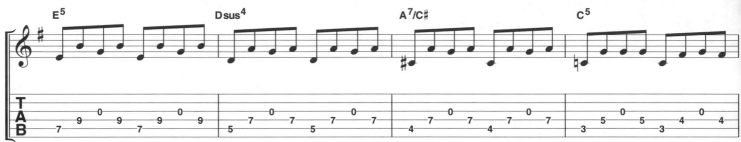

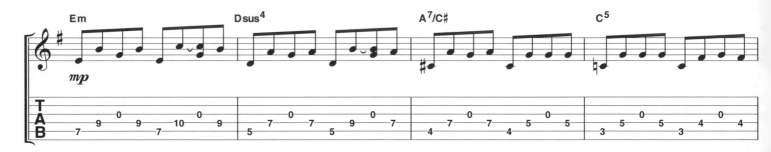

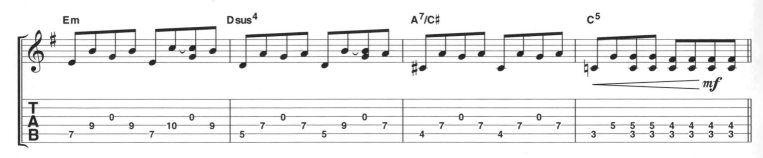

Guitar Grade 4

Secret Place

Ian Woolway

There And Beck

Simon Troup

Guitar Grade 4

Guitar Solo

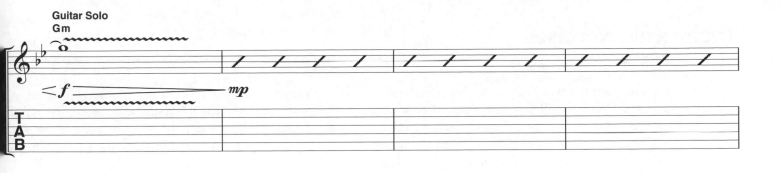

Chordal Accompaniment

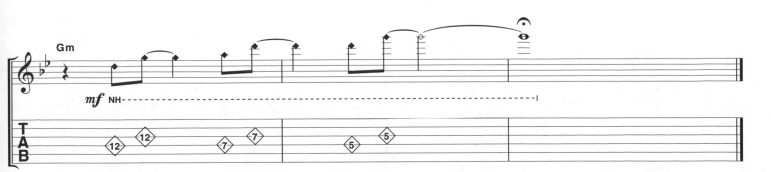

Technical Exercises

In this section, the examiner will ask you to play a selection of exercises drawn from each of the three groups shown below. Groups A and B contain examples of the kinds of scales and arpeggios you can use when playing the pieces. Group C contains a selection of chords commonly used in the pieces. In Group D you will be asked to prepare the riff exercise and play it to the CD backing track. You do not need to memorise the exercises (and can use the book in the exam) but the examiner will be looking for the speed of your response. The examiner will also give credit for the level of your musicality.

Groups A and B should be prepared in the following keys: chromatically from G–B (root note: 6th string) or chromatically from C–E (root note: 5th string). The root note for each exercise is indicated in the example. Groups A, B and C should be played at ♩ = 80. The examiner will give you this tempo in the exam.

Group A: Scales

1. Major scales. G major scale shown: root 6th string

2. Natural minor scales. C♯ natural minor scale shown: root note 5th string

3. Major pentatonic scales. G major pentatonic scale shown: root note 6th string

4. Minor pentatonic scales. D minor pentatonic shown: root note 5th string

5. Blues scales. E blues scale shown: root note 5th string

Group B: Arpeggios

1. Minor ^{7} arpeggios. G minor ^{7} arpeggio shown: root note 6th string

2. Dominant ^{7} arpeggios. A dominant ^{7} arpeggio shown: root note 6th string

Group C: Chords

1. Extended barre chords: to be given as a continuous exercise

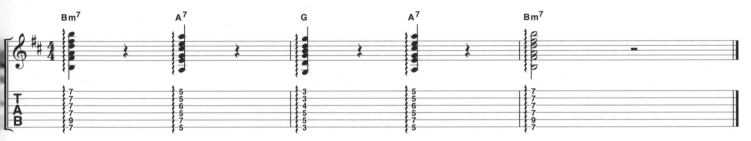

Group D: Riff

In the exam you will be asked to play the following pentatonic riff to the backing track on the CD. The riff shown in bars 1 & 2 should be played in the same shape in bars 3-8. The root note of the pattern to be played is shown in the music in each bar where the chord changes. The tempo is ♩ = 100.

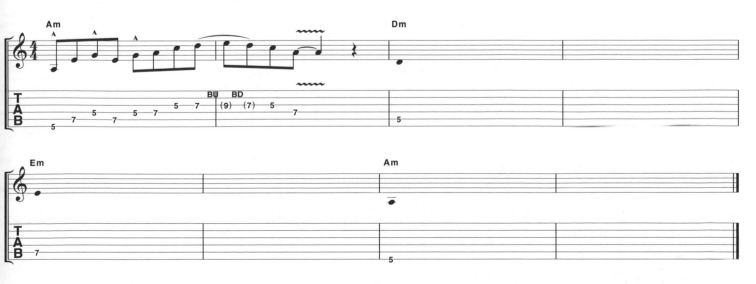

Sight Reading

In this section you have a choice between **either** a sight reading test **or** an improvisation & interpretation test (see facing page). Printed below is the type of sight reading test you are likely to encounter in the exam. At this level there is an element of improvisation. This is in the form of a two bar ending. The piece will be composed in the style of blues, rock, funk or jazz and will have chord symbols throughout. The test is eight bars long. The improvised ending will use chord patterns that have been used in the sight reading part of the test. The examiner will allow you 90 seconds to prepare it and will set the tempo for you on a metronome. The tempo is ♩=80.

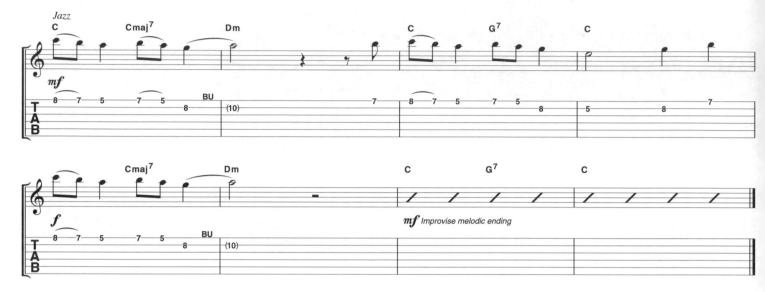

Improvisation & Interpretation

Printed below is an example of the type of improvisation & interpretation test you are likely to encounter in the exam. At this level there is also a small element of sight reading. This takes the form of a two bar chord rhythm at the beginning of the test. You will be asked to play the chords in the given rhythm and continue an improvised line using chords and melody where indicated. This test is given to a backing track lasting eight bars in the style of blues, rock, funk or jazz played by the examiner on CD. You will be allowed 30 seconds to prepare. You will then be allowed to practise through one playing of the test on CD before playing it a second time for the exam. This test is continuous with a one bar count in at the beginning and after the practice session. The tempo is ♩=90.

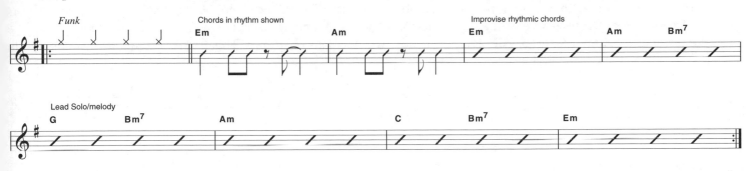

Ear Tests

There are two ear tests in this grade. The examiner will play each test to you twice on CD. You will find one example of each type of test you will be given in the exam printed below.

Test 1: Melodic Recall

You will be asked to play back on your guitar a melody of not more than four bars composed from either the C major or C minor scales. The test may include hammer ons, pull offs and slides. You will be given the tonic note and told the starting note and you will hear the test twice with a drum backing. There will then be a short break for you to practise the test and then the test will recommence. You will play the melody with the drum backing. This test is continuous. The tempo is ♩=80.

Test 2: Chord and Rhythm Recall

You will be asked to play back the four bar rhythmic chord progression on your guitar. You will be told the tonic chord and hear the rhythmic chord progression played twice with a drum backing. There will then be a short break for you to practise the test and then the test will recommence and you will play the rhythmic chord progression to the drum backing. This test is continuous. The tempo is ♩=80.

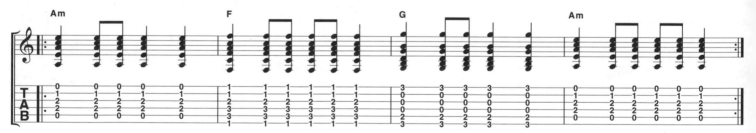

General Musicianship Questions

You will be asked five General Musicianship Questions at the end of the exam. The examiner will ask questions based on pieces you have played in the exam. Some of the theoretical topics can be found in the Technical Exercises.

Topics:

i)   Music theory
ii)   Knowledge of your instrument

The music theory questions will cover the recognition of the following at this grade:

Note pitches	Dynamic markings (*p*, *mp*, *mf*, *f* and *ff*)
Note values	Repeat markings
Rests	Accents, staccato and vibrato
Time Signatures	Hammer on and pull off
Key Signatures	Cresc. and dim.
D.S. and D.C. al Coda	

Knowledge of the construction of the following chord types:

Major	Dominant ^{7}
Minor	Minor ^{7}

The instrument knowledge questions will cover the following topics at this grade:

Plugging into the amplifier and the guitar
Volume and tone adjustments on the guitar
Volume and tone adjustments on the amplifier
Knowledge of one open string tuning method not involving a tuning device

Knowledge of parts of the guitar:

Fretboard, neck, body, tuning pegs, nut, pickups, bridge, pickup selectors, scratchplate and jack socket

Knowledge of main guitar makes.

Knowledge of main pickup types.

Questions on all these topics will be based on pieces played by you in the exam. Tips on how to approach this part of the exam can be found in the Rockschool Companion Guide and on the Rockschool website: *www.rockschool.co.uk.*

The Guru's Guide To Guitar Grade 4

This section contains some handy hints compiled by Rockschool's Guitar Guru to help you get the most out of the performance pieces. Do feel free to adapt the tunes to suit your playing style. Remember, these tunes are your chance to show your musical imagination and personality.

The TAB fingerings are suggestions only. Feel free to use different neck positions as they suit you. Please also note that any solos featured in the full mixes are not meant to be indicative of the standard required for the grade.

Guitar Grade 4 Tunes

Rockschool tunes help you play the hit tunes you enjoy. The pieces have been written by top pop and rock composers and players according to style specifications drawn up by Rockschool.

The tunes printed here fall into two categories. The first category can be called the 'contemporary mainstream' and features current styles in today's charts. The second category of pieces consists of 'roots styles', those classic grooves and genres which influence every generation of performers.

CD full mix track 1, backing track 8: Enough Said

This driving funk track lays down a bold opening chordal theme that calls for a supple picking hand approach and accurate fretting. The solo section gives you the chance to use some of the ideas found in the Technical Exercises. The chord work needs to be picked with control and should contrast dynamically with the palm muted sections.

Composer: Hussein Boon.

CD full mix track 2, backing track 9: Glide On Down

This song is a hip-hop groove that consists mainly of sparse, repeated chords and a repeated riff pattern doubled with the keyboard part. The opening chords are played staccato as indeed is much of the opening melody that follows. These notes should be given clearly and accurately and you should think about shaping the part with variations to make it sound musical. Make the most of the harmonics in the second half and allow them their full values.

Composer: Joe Bennett.

CD full mix track 3, backing track 10: Hold On I'm Going

A classic Motown soul piece echoing the classics of writers such as Holland-DozieriHolland, while the guitar part is reminiscent of Steve Cropper, the Stax house guitarist. The staples of this style are a sharp, bright tone and quite intricate chord-melody patterns that in the original songs served to act as a counterpoint to the singers. The solo section allows you to demonstrate some of Cropper's closely picked stabbed riff ideas.

Composer: Steve Wrigley.

CD full mix track 4, backing track 11: Rage Against Everything

This Nu Metal piece is a song of contrasts. It starts with a relatively quiet, descending riff played in a clear tone. This is followed by an overdriven chord section played very loud indeed. The solo section also allows you to let rip but remember that this is followed immediately by a return to the main theme which is played at the quieter volume and with the clear tone. The section slows to a grand finish.

Composer: Deirdre Cartwright

CD full mix track 5, backing track 12: Secret Place

This is an uncomplicated blues track similar in feel and drive to the famous song 'Hideaway'. The part is played here with a clear tone and with plenty of swinging attack. The palm muting section leads into a twelve bar solo followed by a comped accompaniment over the piano solo before returning to the main theme. A fun track to play and one where you can show off your blues chops.

Composer: Ian Woolway.

CD full mix track 6, backing track 13: There And Beck

Jeff Beck is perhaps the forgotten British guitar hero of the 60s, more commonly remembered for the kitsch 'Hi Ho Silver Lining' than for his sparse, earthy guitar work. Yet his performances merit a second listen as he plays with so much feel and musicality. This track is a tribute to him and features the slides, quarter bends, vibrato, dirty guitar sound and dynamic range that mark out his playing. Have a listen to his version of the Stevie Wonder track, 'Cause We Ended as Lovers'.

Composer: Simon Troup.

CD Musicians:

Guitars: Deirdre Cartwright; John Parricelli; Hussein Boon; Keith Airey
Bass: Henry Thomas
Drums: Noam Lederman; Peter Huntington
Keyboards and programming: Alastair Gavin

Guitar Grade 4 Marking Schemes

The table below shows the marking scheme for the Guitar Grade 4 exam.

ELEMENT	PASS	MERIT	DISTINCTION
Piece 1	13 out of 20	15 out of 20	17+ out of 20
Piece 2	13 out of 20	15 out of 20	17+ out of 20
Piece 3	13 out of 20	15 out of 20	17+ out of 20
Technical Exercises	11 out of 15	12–13 out of 15	14+ out of 15
Either Sight Reading *or* Improvisation & Interpretation	6 out of 10	7–8 out of 10	9+ out of 10
Ear Tests	6 out of 10	7–8 out of 10	9+ out of 10
General Musicianship Questions	3 out of 5	4 out of 5	5 out of 5
Total Marks	**Pass: 65%+**	**Merit: 75%+**	**Distinction: 85%+**

The table below shows the marking scheme for the Guitar Grade 4 Performance Certificate.

ELEMENT	PASS	MERIT	DISTINCTION
Piece 1	14 out of 20	16 out of 20	18+ out of 20
Piece 2	14 out of 20	16 out of 20	18+ out of 20
Piece 3	14 out of 20	16 out of 20	18+ out of 20
Piece 4	14 out of 20	16 out of 20	18+ out of 20
Piece 5	14 out of 20	16 out of 20	18+ out of 20
Total Marks	**Pass: 70%+**	**Merit: 80%+**	**Distinction: 90%+**

Entering Rockschool Exams

Entering a Rockschool exam is easy. Please read through these instructions carefully before filling in the exam entry form. Information on current exam fees can be obtained from Rockschool by ringing 020 8332 6303 or by logging on to our website *www.rockschool.co.uk*.

• You should enter for your exam when you feel ready.

• You can enter for any one of three examination periods. These are shown below with their closing dates.

PERIOD	DURATION	CLOSING DATE
Period A	1st February to 15th March	1st December
Period B	1st May to 31st July	1st April
Period C	23rd October to 15th December	1st October

These dates will apply from 1st September 2006 until further notice

• Please complete the form giving the information required. Please fill in the type and level of exam, the instrument, along with the period and year. Finally, fill in the fee box with the appropriate amount. You can obtain up to date information on all Rockschool exam fees from the website: *www.rockschool.co.uk*. You should send this form with a cheque or postal order (payable to Rockschool Ltd) to the address shown on the order form. **Please also indicate on the form whether or not you would like to receive notification via email.**

• Applications received after the expiry of the closing date may be accepted subject to the payment of an additional fee.

• When you enter an exam you will receive from Rockschool an acknowledgement letter or email containing a copy of our exam regulations.

• Rockschool will allocate your entry to a centre and you will receive notification of the exam, showing a date, location and time as well as advice of what to bring to the centre. We endeavour to give you four weeks' notice of your exam.

• You should inform Rockschool of any cancellations or alterations to the schedule as soon as you can as it is usually not possible to transfer entries from one centre, or one period, to another without the payment of an additional fee.

• Please bring your music book and CD to the exam. You may not use photocopied music, nor the music used by someone else in another exam. The examiner will sign each book during each examination. You may be barred from taking an exam if you use someone else's music.

• You should aim to arrive for your Grade 4 exam fifteen minutes before the time stated on the schedule.

• Each Grade 4 exam is scheduled to last for 20 minutes. You can use a small proportion of this time to tune up and get ready.

• Two to three weeks after the exam you will receive a copy of the examiner's mark sheet. Every successful player will receive a Rockschool certificate of achievement.